Seth Fluker   At Water

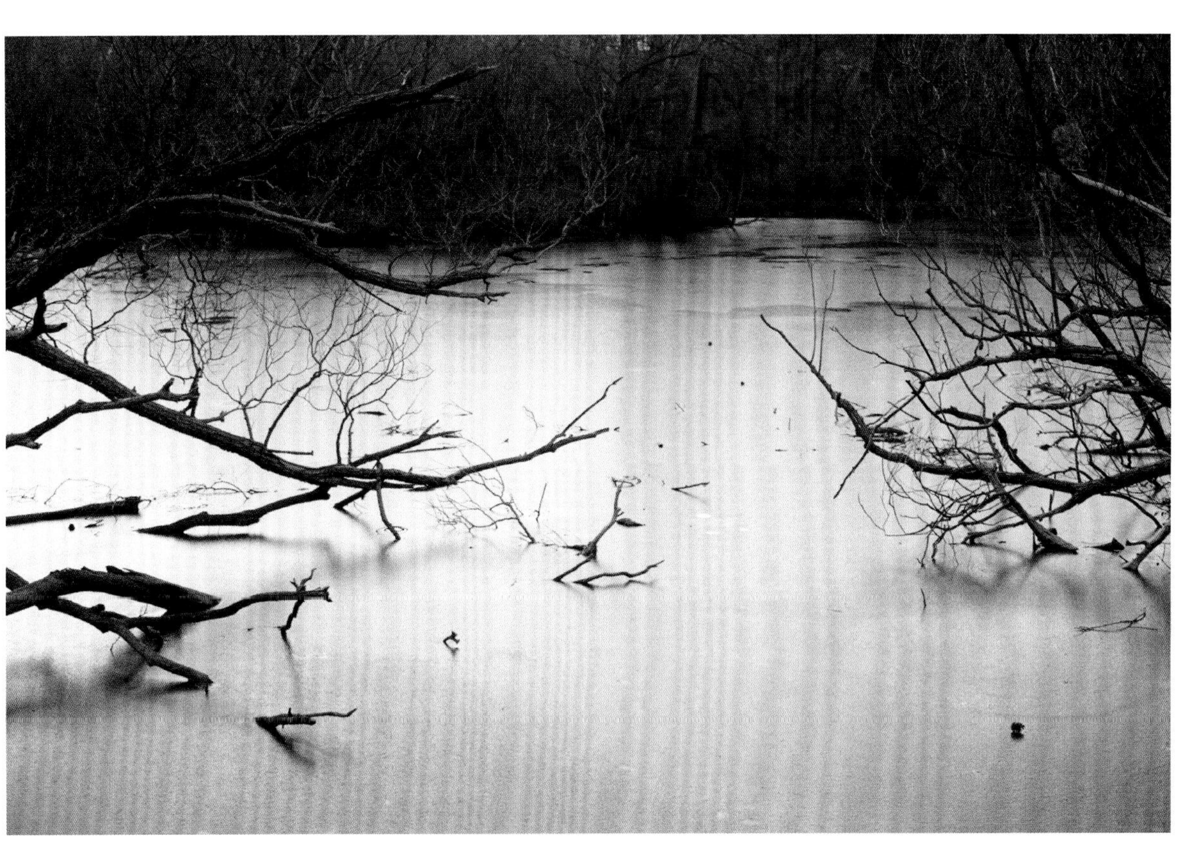

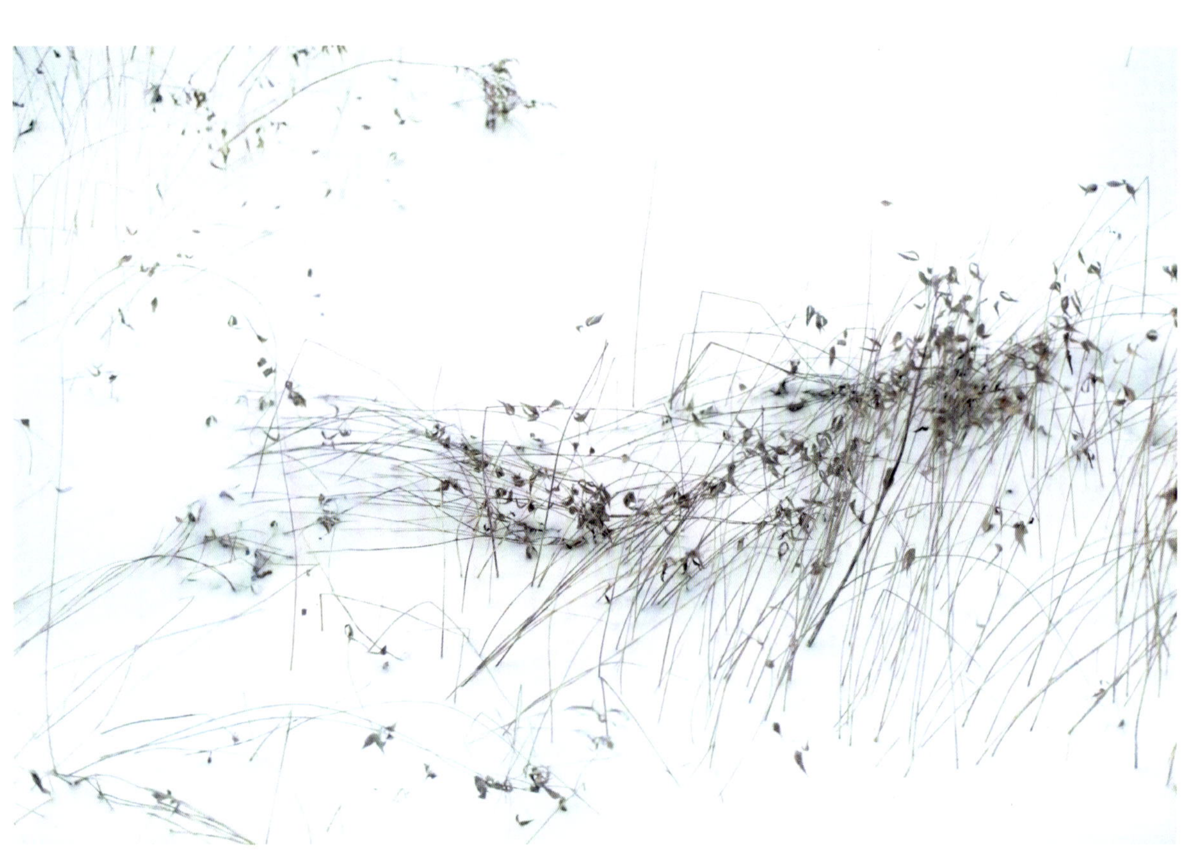

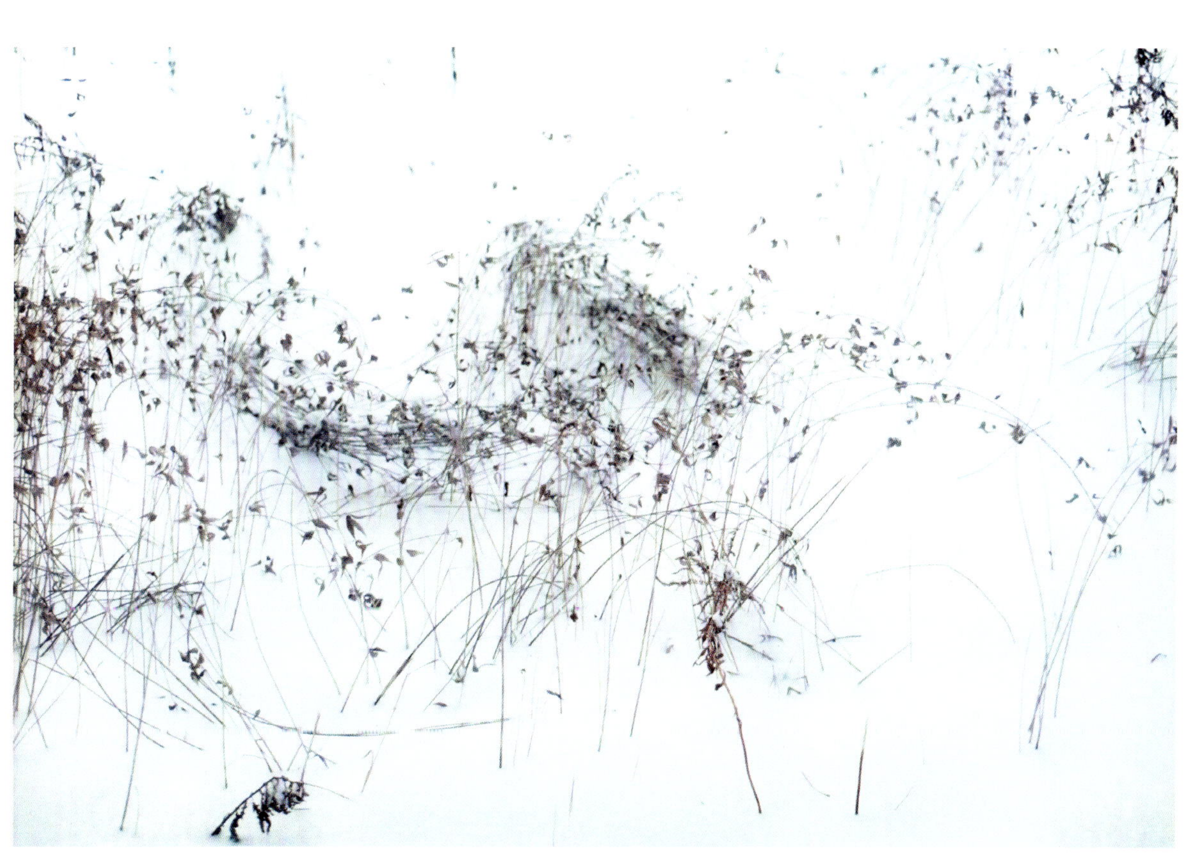

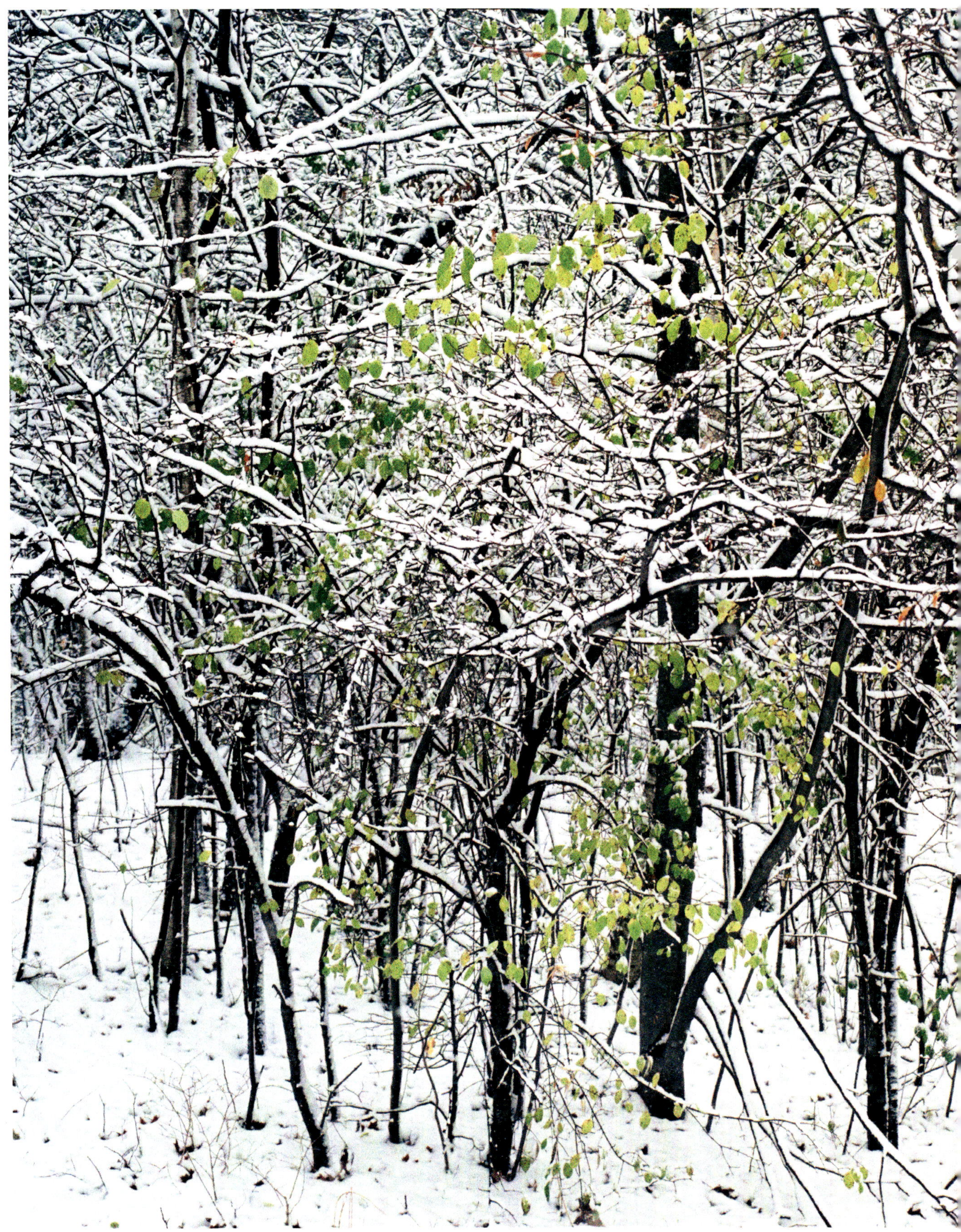

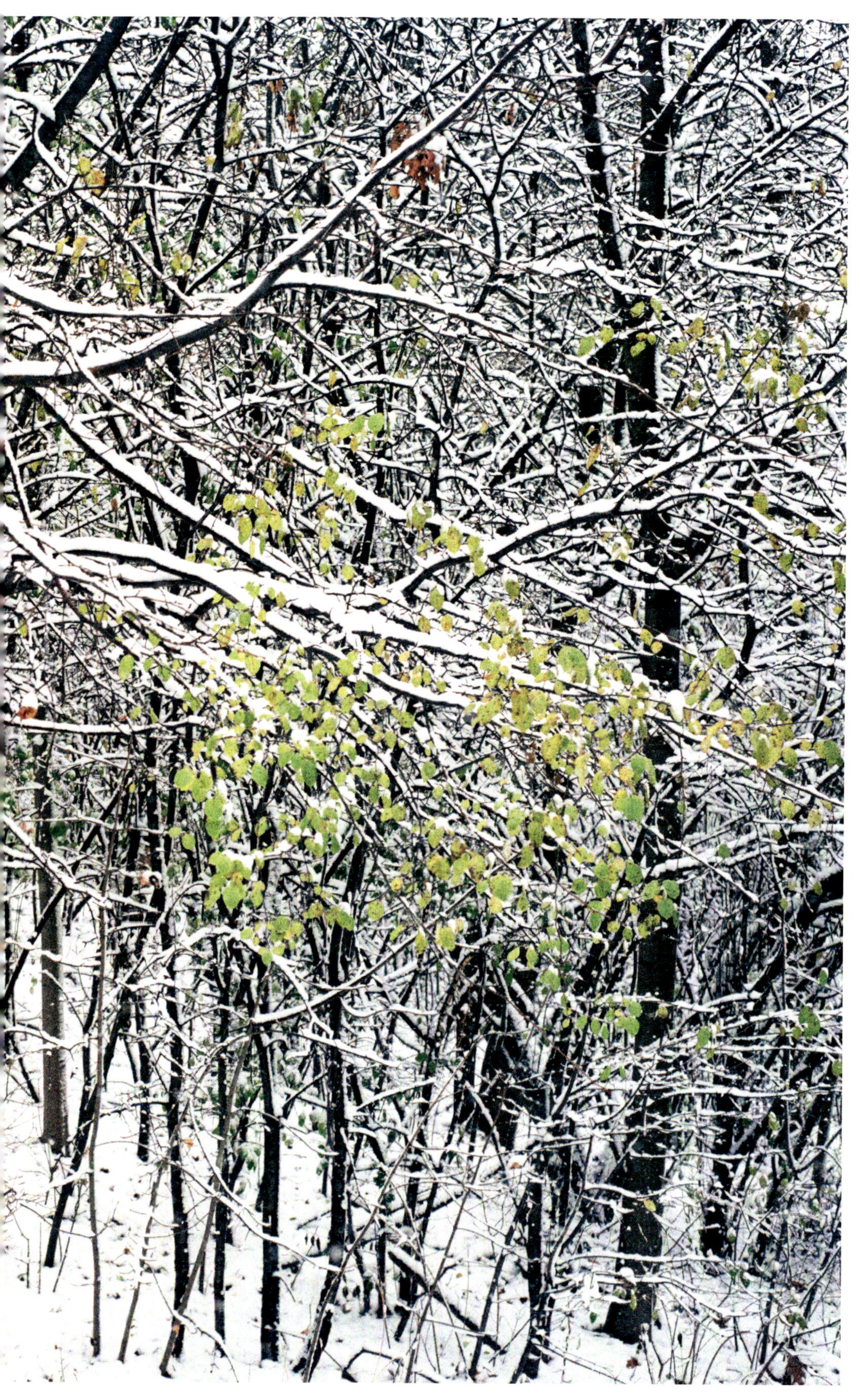

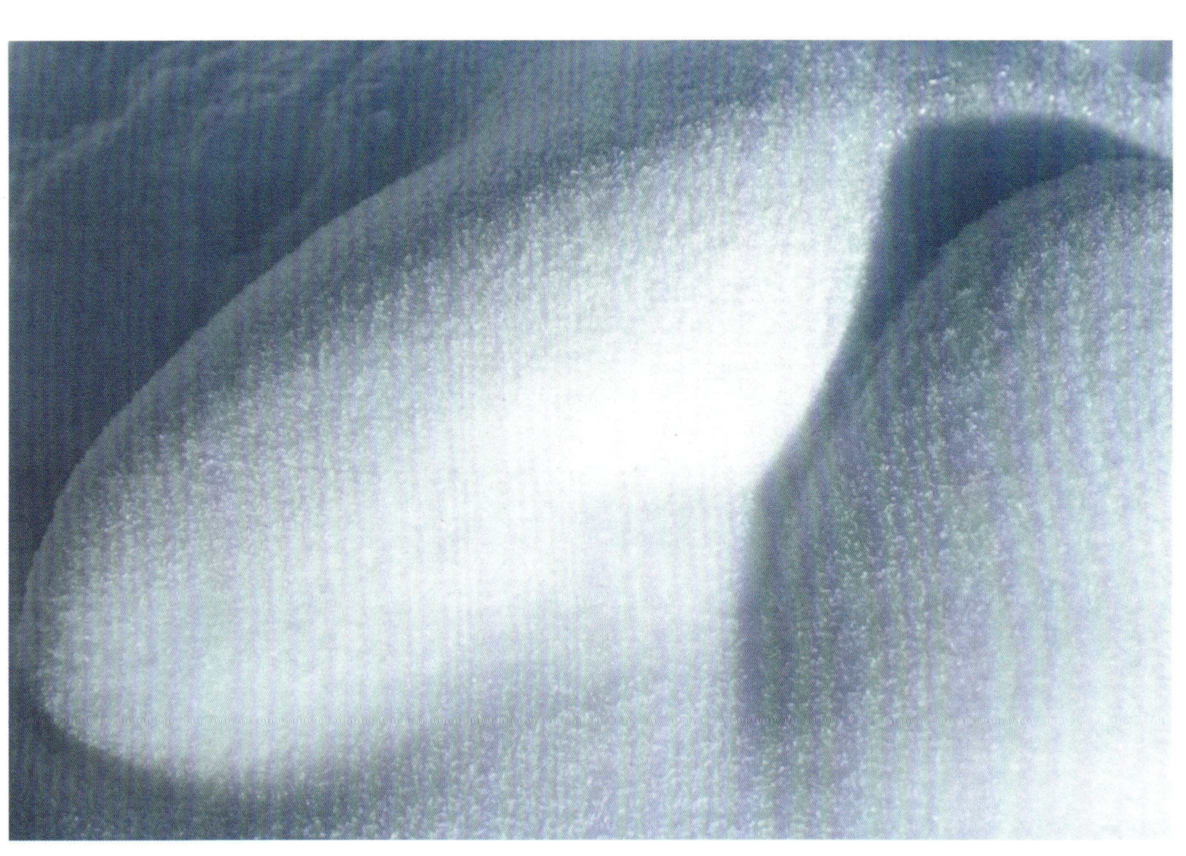

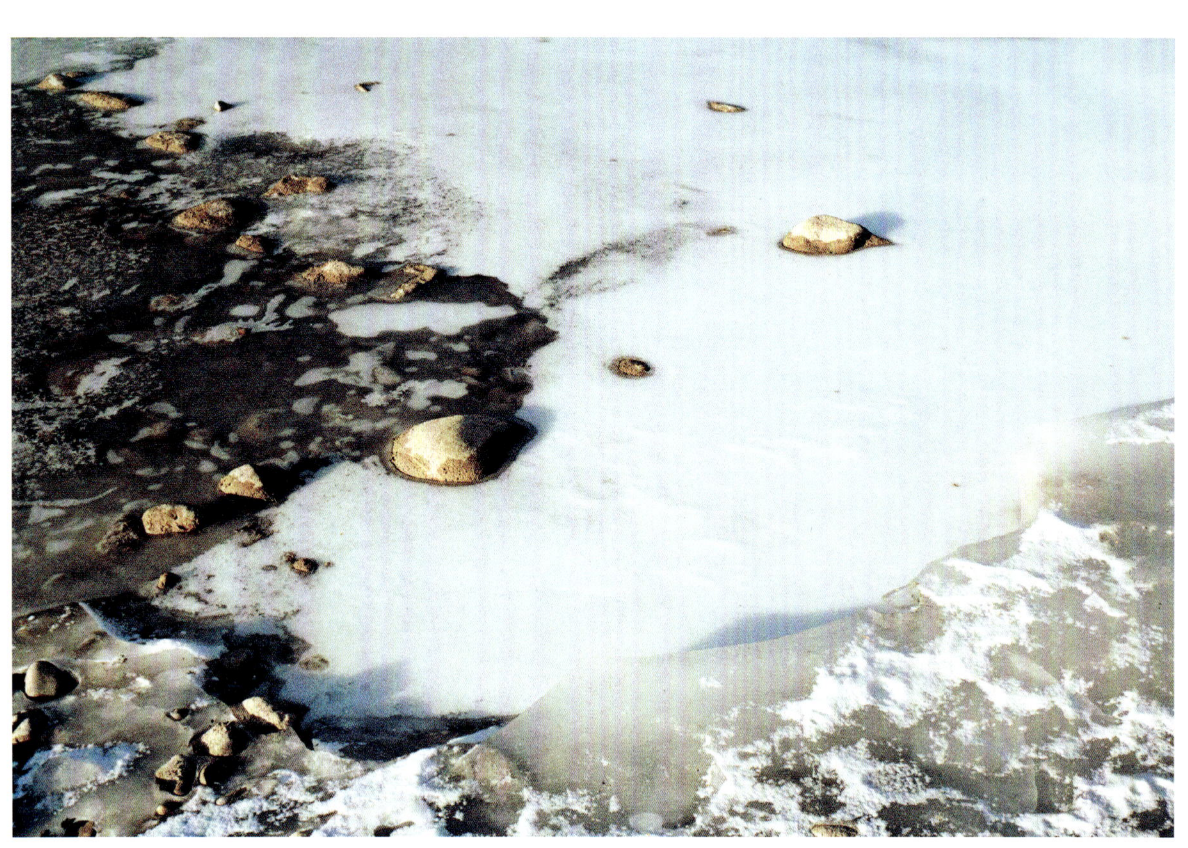

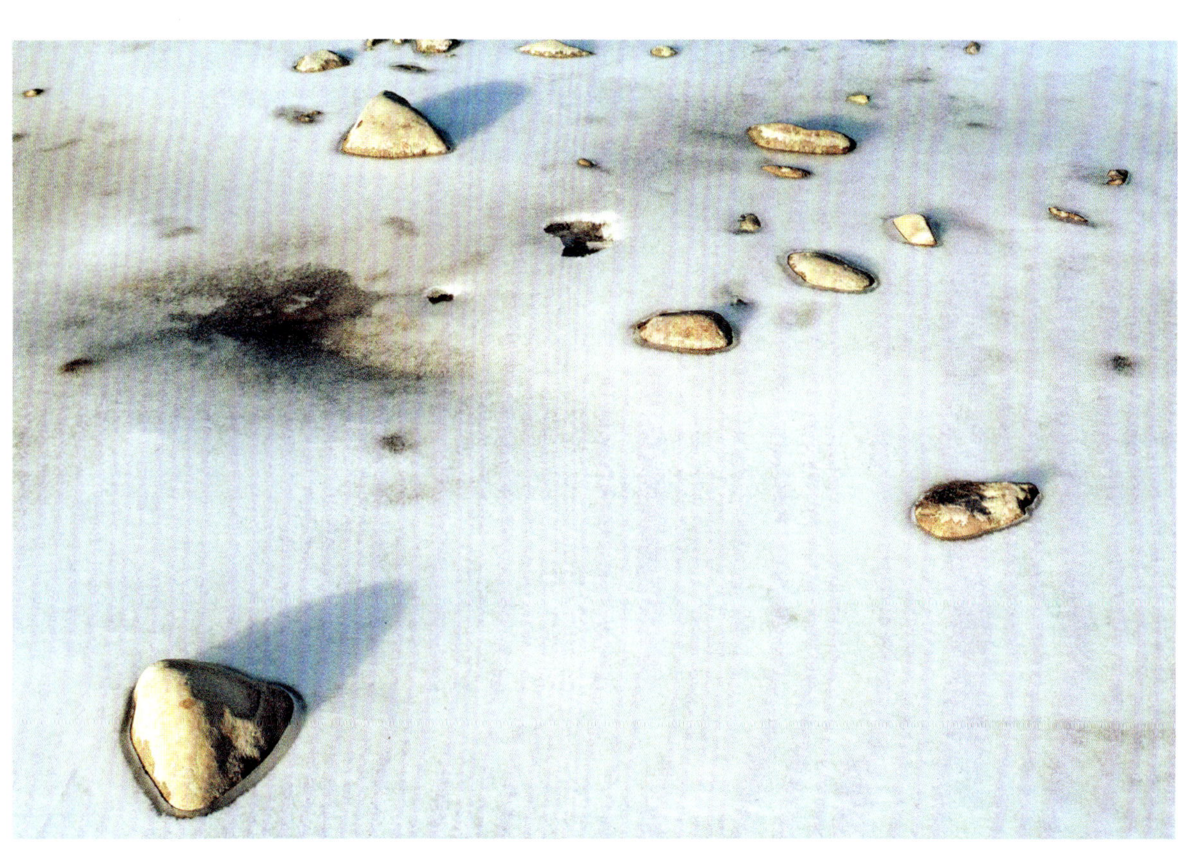

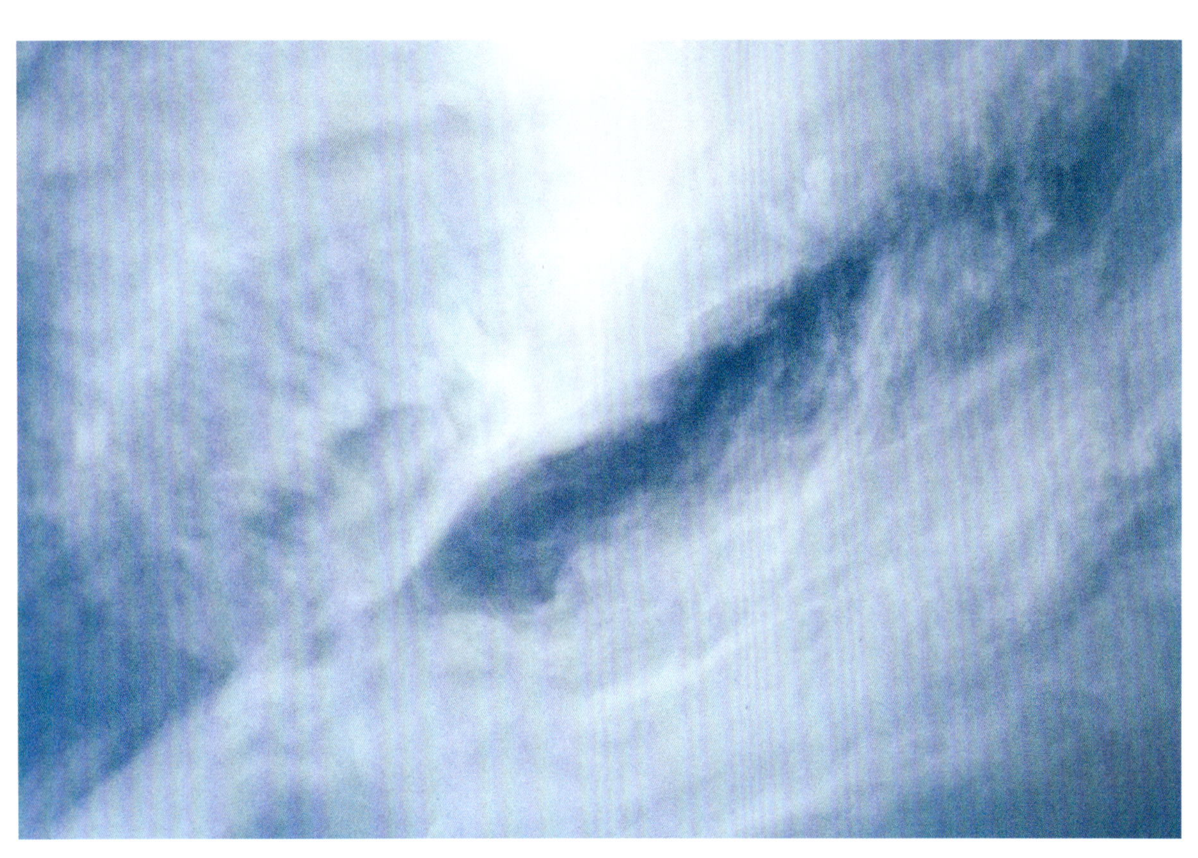

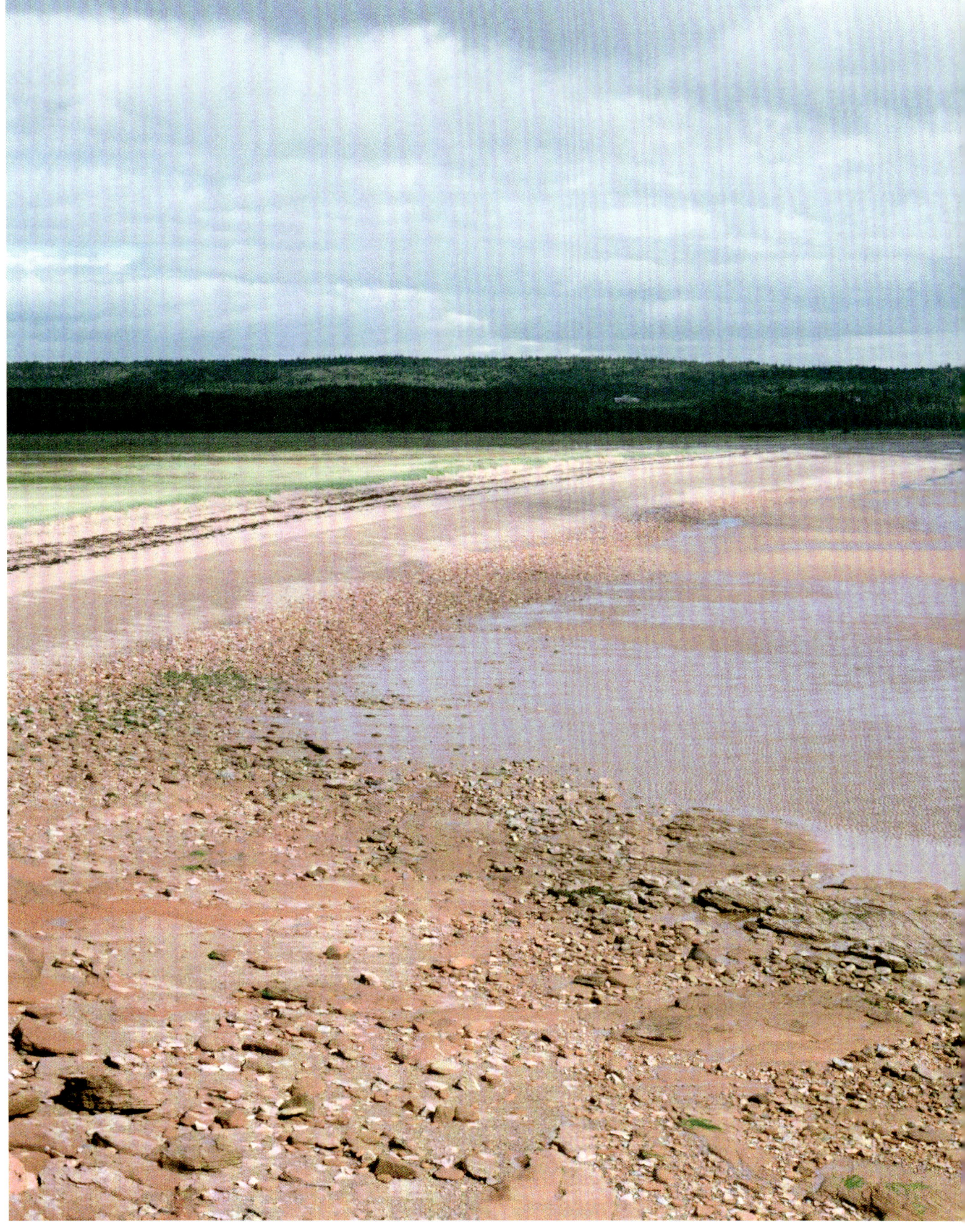

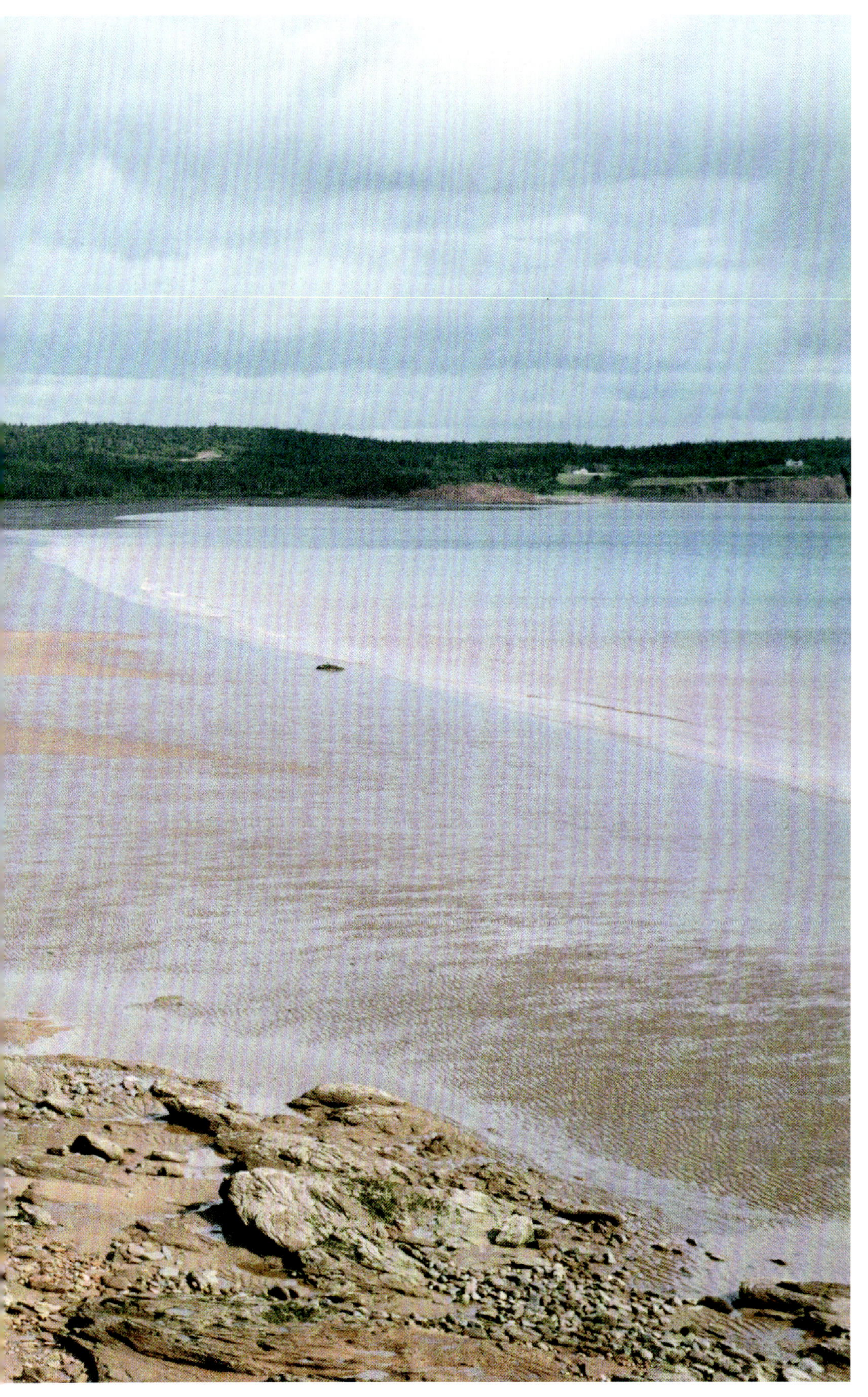

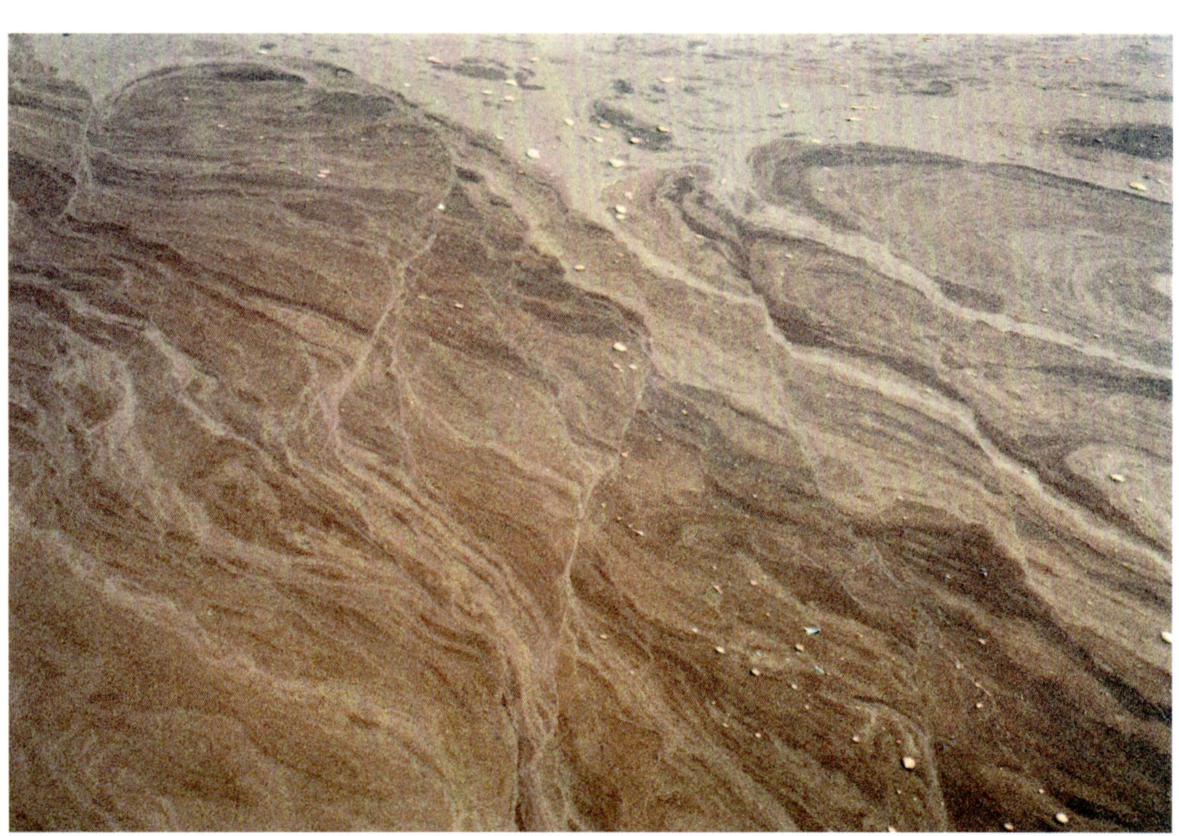

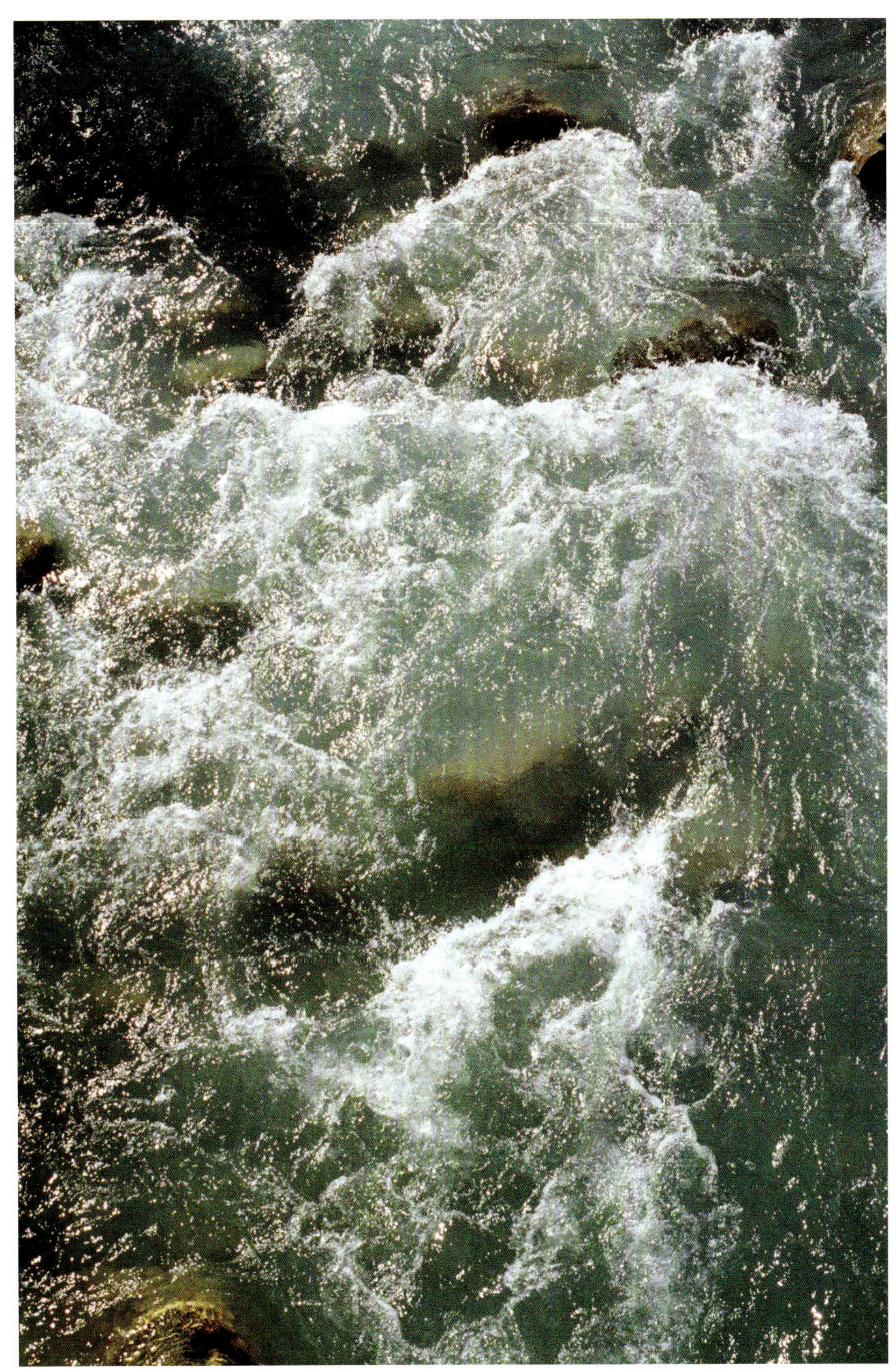

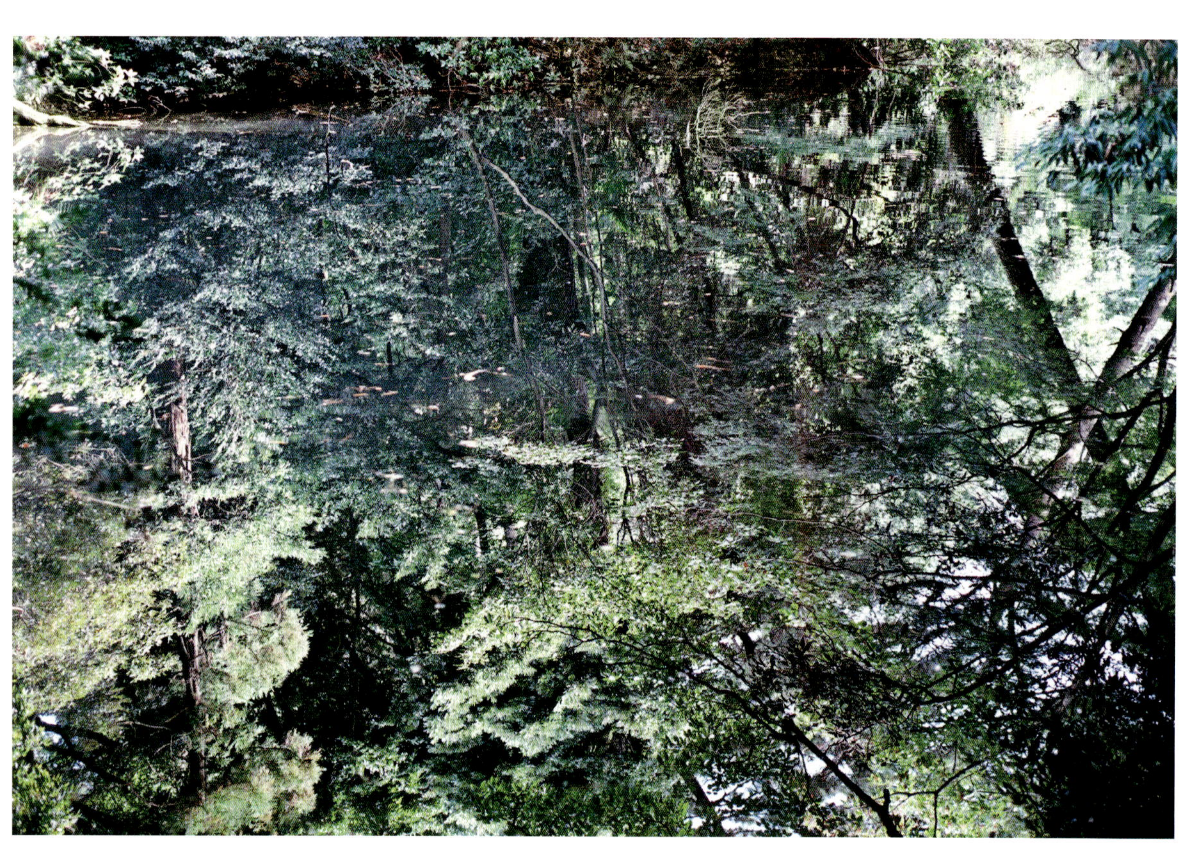

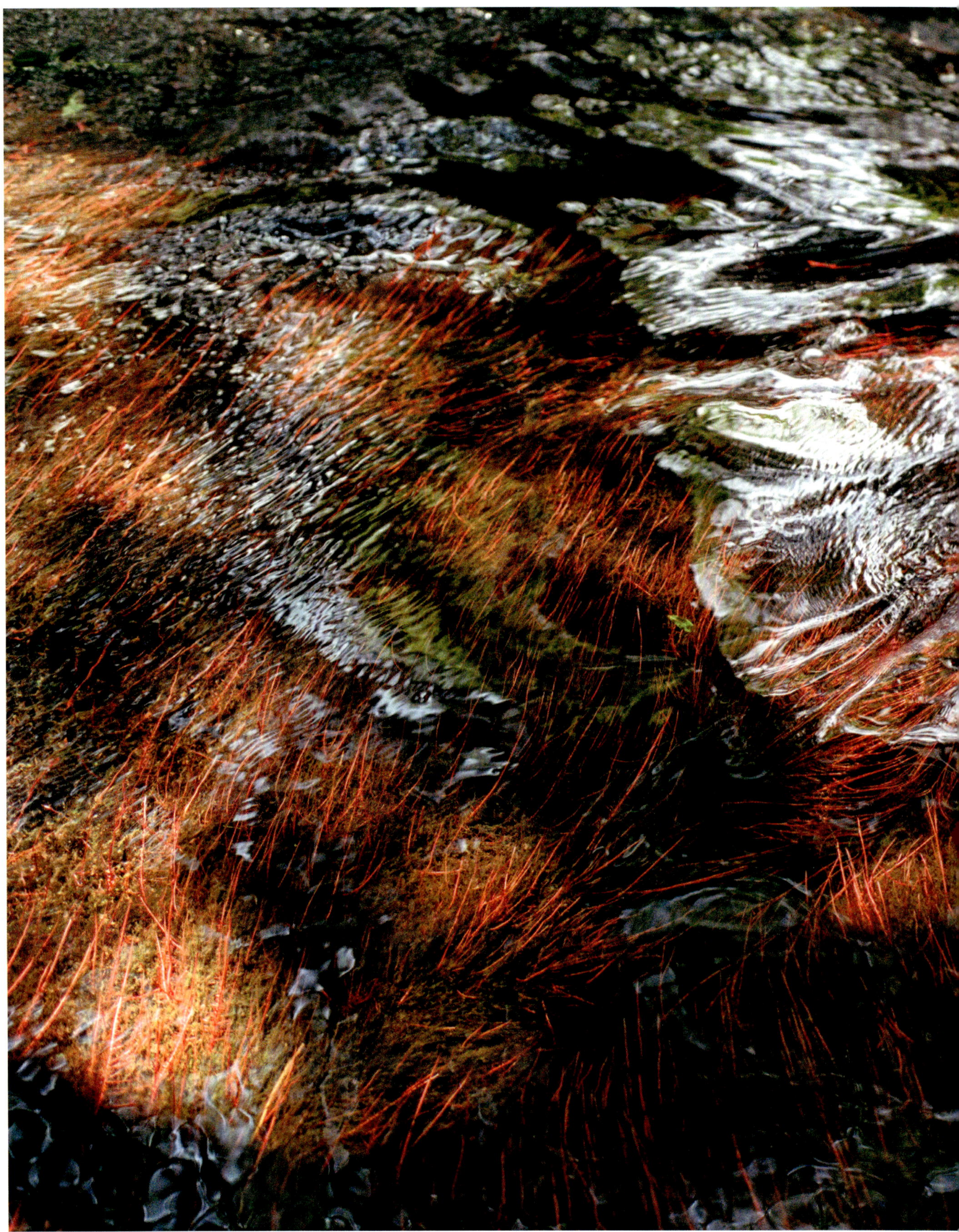

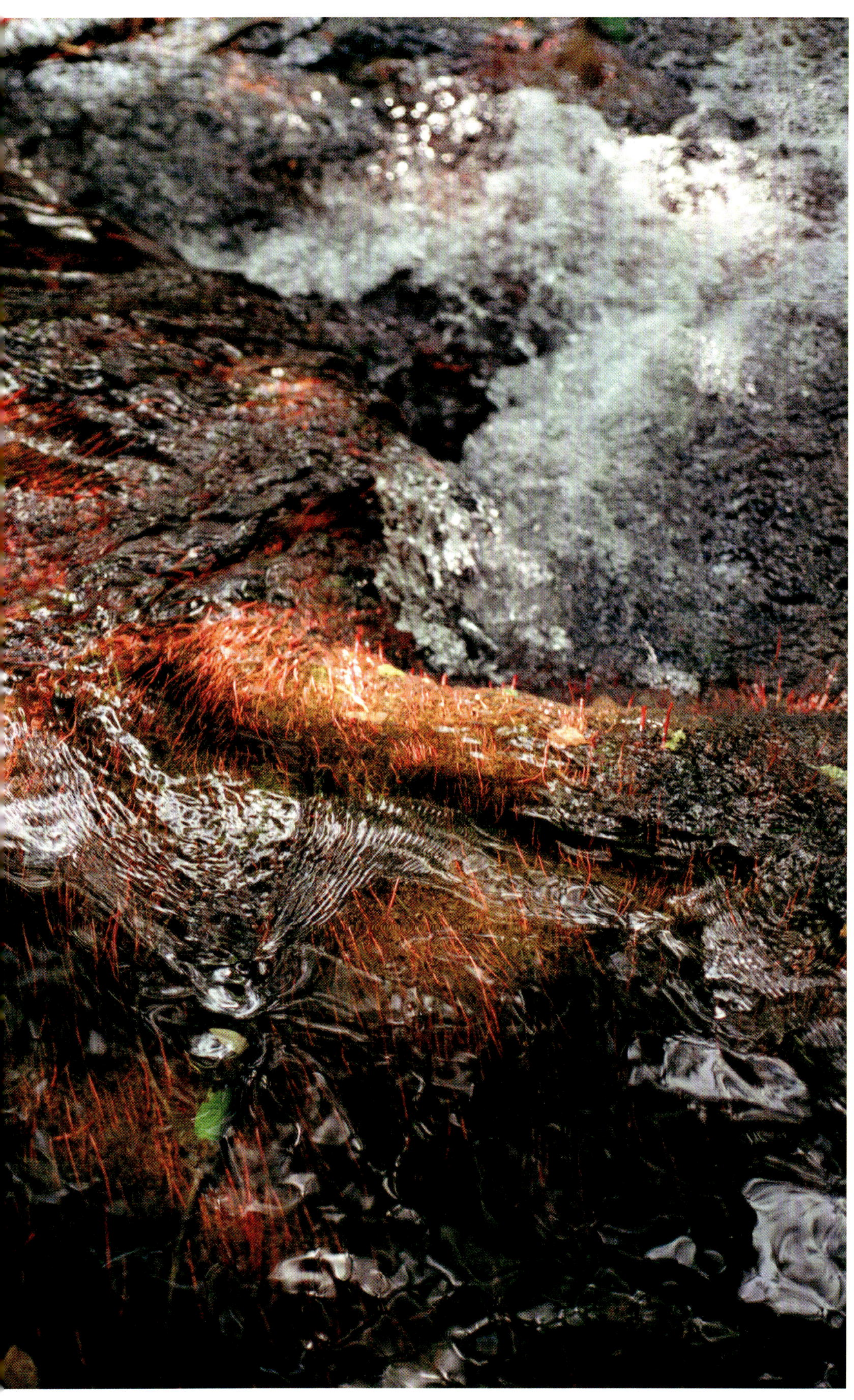

Upper Duck Pond, Toronto, 2020

The Queensway Path, Toronto, 2021

Spring Road, Toronto, 2020

Powder, Bragg Creek, 2019

Elbow River (Sandy Beach), Calgary, 2019

Partially Cloudy, Whistler, 2018

Waterside Beach, New Brunswick, 2016

Water Lapping, New Brunswick, 2016

Rapids, Fitzsimmons Creek, Whistler, 2019

Pond, Shinjuku Gyoen National Garden, Tokyo, 2016

Burble, Calgary, 2021

Seth Fluker
At Water

Published by Hassla
Edition of 300 copies

ISBN 978-1-940881-53-9